101 Affirmations

Women's Affirmations for a Healthier Belief System

Jaida Burch

Affirmation

[/ˌafərˈmāSH(ə)n/] noun

The act of confirming something to be true; a written or oral statement that confirms something is true.

Table of Contents

Foundational Affirmations

I am deserving of the life
I desire to experience.

I am worthy of every good thing
that comes my way.

I believe in myself, fearlessly and
relentlessly.

I am happy.

I am healthy.

I am wealthy.

I am fulfilled.

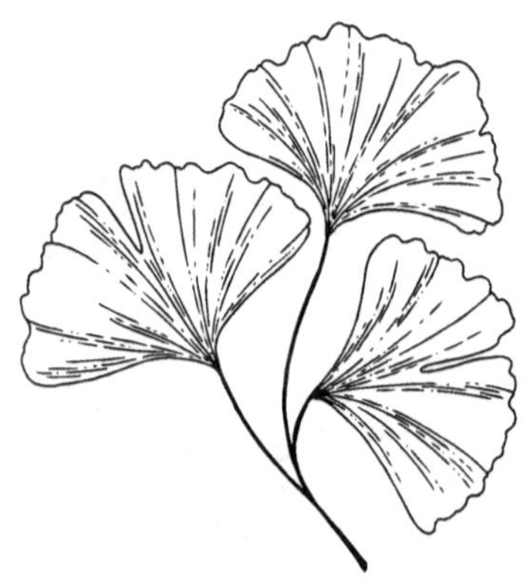

An abundant life is my birthright.

I am the operant power in my life.

Life is not happening to me, but through me.

4

I am the source of my
own stability.

I am the source of my own
happiness.

I am the source of my own
peace.

I am the source of my own
love.

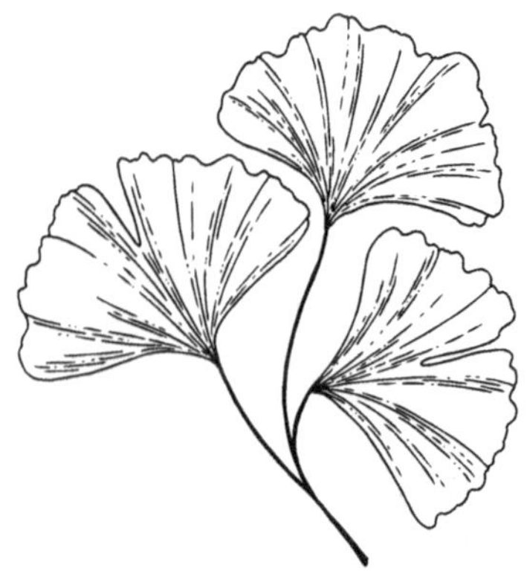

I release resistance from
the things I can't
control.

What is for me is already mine,
how long it takes depends on me.

If I want it and I believe it, I got
it.

My past does not define
me.

I create my future, and will learn
to reminisce as though I've
experienced it.

I will come to anticipate
good things.

I am a powerhouse.

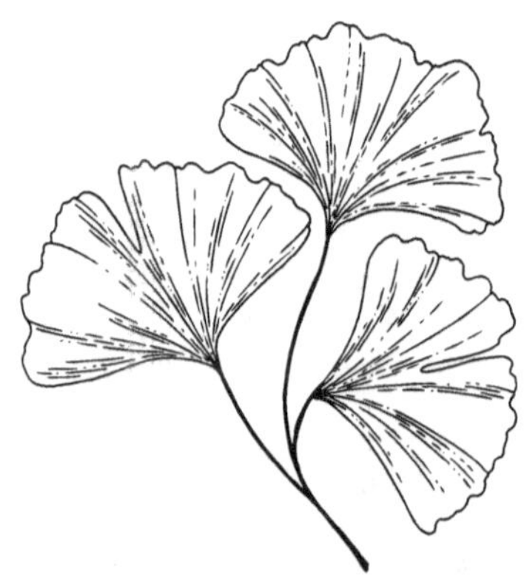

My body is my temple, I
keep her well.

The universe bends and shapes
itself around me.

Everyday is a new opportunity to
grow.

8

Self-Love Affirmations

I radiate beauty, love,
and grace.

I do not chase, I attract.

I choose to love myself more and
more everyday.

I choose to stop
apologizing for being
me.

I am whole on my own, no one
can complete me.

My talents are endless, I
never cease to amaze myself.

My imperfections are what
make me perfect.

I deserve good things,
happiness and joy are
my birthright.

I am unaffected by the
judgement and negativity from
others.

I grow through everything I go
through.

I am enough.

I am wanted.

I am beautiful.

I am unforgettable.

The woman I'm
becoming makes me
proud.

I forgive myself.

I uphold my boundaries.

14

It is okay for me to take
up space.

I do not need outside approval or
validation.

It is okay for me to have
wants and needs.

My best is enough, I do not
deserve burnout.

I am secure within
myself.

I respect myself and the
decisions that I make.

I am not my past, or the things
that have happened to me.

Motivational Affirmations

I do not compare myself
to others, it is the thief
of joy.

I am a limitless being.

I am always successful.

I never lose, I either win
or learn.

The answers are always inside of
me, I just have to be willing to
look.

Opportunities are always
flowing towards me.

I possess every quality I need
for success.

I am unstoppable.

I am getting better and better
everyday.

I always find motivation to get
things done.

I am living with
abundance.

I am an inspiration to people
around me.

I am focused, nothing
knocks me off my path.

I wake up knowing that it's
always going to be a good
day.

I am grateful for
everything in my life.

I use obstacles as a source of
motivation.

Transformations and miracles
are occurring in my life everyday.

I accept myself for who I
am and that is my peace.

Walking away from unhealthy
things is okay.

I stick to what matters and
let go of what doesn't.

I do what makes me happy,
even if others don't approve.

Wealth Affirmations

I attract money easily
and effortlessly.

I am a money magnet.

Wealth always flows into my
life.

I am on my way to
becoming wealthy.

I create abundance with
my thoughts.

I see abundance all around me.

I breathe in abundance.

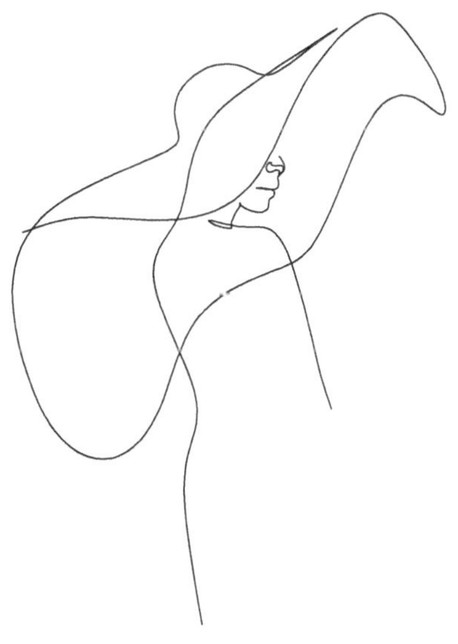

I allow prosperity to
flow into my life.

Money is currency and currency
is energy; energy is always
flowing.

My finances are increasing.

I am the master of my
wealth.

I enjoy managing my
money.

I control money, money does
not control me.

I have a healthy relationship with
money.

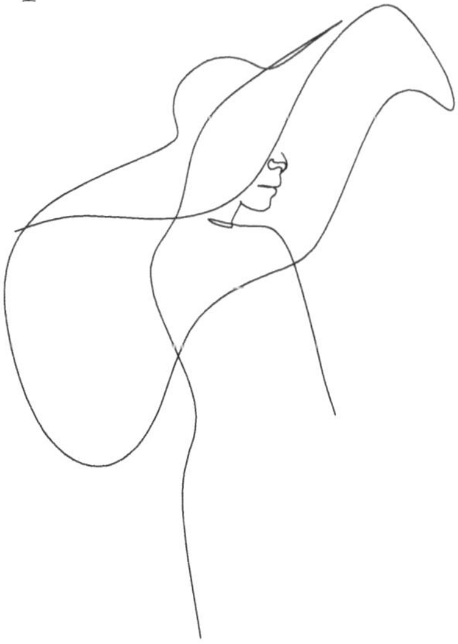

I am in control of my
spending.

Financial success is my
birthright.

By choosing to build wealth
today, I create a better
tomorrow.

I choose to be responsible
with my finances.

Luxury is my birthright
and I get to choose what
luxury means to me.

I have the power to be debt-free.

I am grateful to be able to
manifest money into my life.

Personal Affirmations

Create Your Own Affirmations

The next few pages will allow you to create fourteen of your own personalized affirmations.

These personal affirmations utilize the art of written and spoken words, which help us create our futures.

Be intentional, mindful, and precise when creating these affirmations as words and their meanings produce powerful results.

Last, but most importantly, take this time to dig deep into who you are, your limiting beliefs, and where you want to be. Use these affirmations to align to that being.

Pick four words below that you struggle with the most. Use them in affirmations that best suit you.

Forgiveness Love Confidence
Trust Anxiety Fear Family
Failure Relationships Faith

1. ______________________________

____

2. ______________________________

____

3. ______________________________

____

4. ______________________________

____

Pick three words below that you struggle with the most. Use them in affirmations that best suit you.

Career Job Purpose
Talent Opportunity Skill Niche
School Business Path

1. ________________________________

____

2. ________________________________

____

3. ________________________________

____

Pick four words below that you struggle with the most. Use them in affirmations that best suit you.

Joy Peace Stable
Abundant Happy Grateful
Excited Proud Relaxed

1. ____

____

2. ____

____

3. ____

____

4. ____

____

Pick three words below that you struggle with the most. Use them in affirmations that best suit you.

Can Will Do
Am Have Does Has
Is Are Could

1. _______________________________

____

2. _______________________________

____

3. _______________________________

____

Closing Notes

Affirmations should be a part of everyone's daily, and even nightly, routines. We speak things, people, opportunities, and events into our lives every day, so why not start being intentional with it? Be accountable for the role you play in creating the life you desire to live.

While it may sound awkward at first, choosing three affirmations and repeating them to yourself in the mirror creates a powerful sense of self. Doing this every day will not only create a habit, but bring about changes in your reality. Don't knock it 'til you try it.

Keep affirming, until you become.

Love,

Jaida

www.ingramcontent.com/pod-product-compliance
Lightning Source LLC
Chambersburg PA
CBHW070616160726

48003CB00005B/2307